EVERYTHING THAT HURT US BECOMES A GHOST

EVERYTHING THAT HURT US BECOMES A GHOST

Poems

SAGE RAVENWOOD

Gallaudet University Press
Washington, DC

Gallaudet University Press
gupress.gallaudet.edu

Gallaudet University Press is located on the
traditional territories of Nacotchtank and Piscataway.

Printed in the United States of America

ISBN 978-1-954622-22-7 (paperback)
ISBN 978-1-954622-23-4 (ebook)

Library of Congress Cataloging-in-Publication Data
Names: Ravenwood, Sage, author.
Title: Everything that hurt us becomes a ghost : poems / Sage Ravenwood.
Description: Washington : Gallaudet University Press, [2023]. | Summary: "Everything That Hurt Us Becomes a Ghost is a poetry collection by deaf Indigenous (Cherokee) author Sage Ravenwood. In it, Ravenwood paints a complex portrait of trauma, survival, and navigating the world as a late deafened person"-- Provided by publisher.
Identifiers: LCCN 2023013705 (print) | LCCN 2023013706 (ebook) | ISBN 9781954622227 (paperback) | ISBN 9781954622234 (ebook)
Subjects: LCSH: Ravenwood, Sage--Poetry. | Deaf women--Poetry. | LCGFT: Autobiographical poetry. | Poetry.
Classification: LCC PS3618.A936 E94 2023 (print) | LCC PS3618.A936 (ebook) | DDC 811/.6--dc23/eng/20230526
LC record available at https://lccn.loc.gov/2023013705
LC ebook record available at https://lccn.loc.gov/2023013706

∞ This paper meets the requirements of ANSI/NISO Z39.48–1992 (Permanence of Paper).

Cover description: White background with two black feathers, one at the top right, and one on the middle left. On the top left there are traces of blood. At the center of the cover, lowercase title in dark text reads, everything that hurt us becomes a ghost, with slightly blurred text on the right. Underneath, between two traces of blood, in small dark gray text reads the subtitle: poems. At the bottom of the cover, in dark text reads: Sage Ravenwood.

Cover design by Eric C. Wilder.

CONTENTS

III: Twilight's Lonely Cleave

IV: Soft Animal

V: Season's Betrayal

VI: Leave the Braid
(Abnegations)

NOTE FROM THE AUTHOR

This book is based on my own experiences growing up in an Indigenous household with a Cherokee mother and a German father, with depictions of how her religious fanaticism and his alcoholism devoured my family whole. Inside the poems I explore my identity as an Indigenous deaf woman finding her way through life.

I'm a domestic violence and sexual abuse survivor who rescues animals the way I wish someone had rescued me. Some of the poems in this collection include depictions of abuse.

The epigraph on the following page is a nod toward survivors who have been bullied into silence regarding their abuse. When we tell our truth and expose that which hurt us, we reckon with the trauma that has instilled itself in our lives. This book is my story.

GLOSSARY OF CHEROKEE WORDS

Atsisonvnv	Hurt
Asgina	Malevolent spirit
Ani Tsutsa	Origin Cherokee story of the Pleiades and the Pine
Elohi	Earth
Golanv	Raven
Sgidolige	I'm sorry or forgive me
Sgwanehlanv	You are my creator
Svnoyi	Night
Uk'tena	A serpent with wings on its back and horns on its head
Unetlanvhi	Great Spirit
Didanetliyvedi	Trade

Silence is either the loudest scream or the most profound reckoning.

I: Resonance

AMONG THE MISSING

There's no flesh between love and pain
Lover's hands clasped painfully tight
Twin shadows   Never one without the other
Thin transparency between two palms
Holding on   Holding back
        Grip crushing   dying to let go
I used to miss you   before I met me
Love was among the missing   buried under want
A wraparound porch circling a heart
House sternum with evergreen ribbed shades
        overlooking a lake of gastric acid
You swallowed me whole and here I sit
Porch nesting   Birding molting scraps
        twig braiding a nest into a spit chest plaster
Hair breeze floating with each inhale   exhale
Lung balloons choking me out of home
Birdcaged misogyny   Mine and only mine lair
Pecking my heart for sustenance   feeding our lies
        eggs hope laid   spilling out of my nest
Winged scapula   blades filleting my shoulders
Wish appendages sprouting downy plumate
Pain grown with each house of you gasp
Wings fleshing out   fluttering
        beak flounced and straightened
I wrap claws around the porch railing   caw outrage
Fly   aerial diving a black winged coughing fit
Feather scratched   talon shredding
        until your mouth unhinges wide
Taking flight   flown from a mouth of only yours
Never ours   yours or mine   missing or met
Between love and pain a thin membrane
stretched to breaking open my leaving

A NAME IS A HAUNTING

Placing a heart in a deli meat slicer
Thin slices of memory folding in on itself
Sandwiched in between loaves of missing you
Swallowed whole by an open grave
As ethereal hands guide my face side to side
Searching the crowd for the one
Who answers your name
Did you send an email to keep hope alive
An alphabet dance of hurt
Branding my skin with loss and not you
It's never you no matter how often
The sound splices my lips in bitten denial
Spelling out never wanted this ending
Or you to orbit my thoughts
In the letting go to save me

SAY LOVE

Birds regurgitate food for young chicks
        You're not a bird   don't swallow love
Remove the ache from four letters
Whisper mute tongue less
Peach limb whip against will
        Bloody dripping I don't want to
Say love as if it's not a serrated knife in hand
A bloody chunk of raw meat
        force fed to a vegetarian
Counting seconds between each belched syllable
Biting fingers nails to the quick   ground
between teeth   Expectations   jaw sore   wired shut
Strangled whimper   neck swollen   breathe
        Say it back before you choke
Yanked strands of hair   throat knitted
Teeth pulling smile   toothless benevolence
Scream quietly through a drought of tears
Drooling emotion into a mournful lake
All of life   can't put me
back together again   Deaf ears
never hear you say   Say love   I can't
I cut the words out of my throat
        mafia neck-tied my tongue
You can have everyone else's   balm the idiocy
Words falling easy from lips
        having never tasted   savored the cost

HARBINGER

She saw the flame flit by out of the corner of her eye
Dancing indelicately from branch to branch
Brilliant red   a chokeberry with wings
    Red-orange bill   black masked eyes
A bank robbing cardinal with a punk mohawk for a crest
She laughed   If only she could hear the badass songbird
The mewling tabby beside her shoved his head in her palm
    Her finger accidentally rubbing against an incisor
Not unlike last summer when the strange beasty
    crawled under the book she read in the yard
      laying claim to her lap and her
She watched the crimson joy fluttering low   Curious
By the fourth day she saw him everywhere
There wasn't a mate   a tawny brown likeness
    with red tinged wings rocking his world
Always flying low within eyesight
Perched on a tether wire
    Hovering over the mailbox
    Dancing a gig on a low stump in the crab apple tree
If he had a message from the dead
    there was nothing left to say or haunt her
Love and luck didn't go hand in hand either   not for her
Whatever the Indigenous believed
    Catholics corroded it by making the cardinal
    A *hinge* to the church   Not a crimson bird
        servicing the lovelorn luck of the dead
This is stupid   it's a beautiful albeit confused bird
    looking for a mate and a place to call home
Shaking whatever silly notions she had from her head
    startled   she swore her deaf ears
    heard the crunch first

Sitting down hard on the steps
she watched in stupefied horror as her last summer
strange beasty landed on all fours   blood dripping
blood red feathers   floating
carrying the cardinal   head flopping   off in his mouth
All the what ifs settled with a thud
Now she'll never know if a bird was something more
She got up to grab a shovel to bury her harbinger
This at least makes perfect sense
Creator should have known love or any notion of luck
would haunt such a tiny body
For a moment she's not sure
If she's talking about herself or the bird

WALLPAPERED

Her eyes trace the outline of the Manchurian Cranes.
A lone red patch on black heads with long olive bills;
Lithe snow-white necks and bodies with black tipped wings.
 Wings always spread wide, always in flight.
 Backdropped by gold-spun clouds over muted
  dark blue beginning to fade twilight skies.
An ash brown shawl of feathers for the females.
Dark brown eyes like hers always watching, staring back
 into hers; bewitching accompaniment.
She noticed every exquisite detail. He didn't.
There's jagged scratch marks in places.
Did the cat sense movement among the birds in flight,
 a fluttering desire to be free of the wall, this place?
Even torn beauty prevailed, unlike her plain, uninteresting.
This was visual euphoria. How could she be wallpaper
 with a crane's grace and mysticism. Immortality
  trapped by paste to a wall, unnoticed eye candy.
Her long thin fingers tease the edges, torn bits from the scratches,
gentle at first, turning to frenzied clawing until blood dripped
 anointing the crimson crowns of multiple heads.
Still they were not free. Hurry, before he returns.
Upend the odds and ends kitchen drawer,
 crawl on hands and knees through the clutter,
  find the wide putty knife, butcher blade wide.
Within minutes wings quiver among trailing
 strips of wallpaper. *Fly, get away from here. Go now!*
Here and there a dark brown eye touches her cheek.
When finished the wall sat empty of life.
Sticky gouged patches of nothingness.
Now she would blend in. In quiet abandon
 she felt something tickle softly;
Did she swallow feathers attempting to free the birds?

The rattling kar-roo crane's call beckoned.
Spitting out pieces of wallpaper, dropping
    the bloody putty knife from her nail torn hand,
a not so plain woman
walked out the door to find her cranes.

I'M NOT THE BRANCH

I hold up a hand as if to wave
Middle and ring fingers arrowed down   rocking
    horns with the thumb sticking out
What remains is supposed to be the ASL sign for love
My thumb   index   and pinky touch yours
Fingers air kissing in signage   *Hello, I love you*
But you and I are different signs   black birds circling
Lock thumbs and wave your hands
    we're wings in flight   skydiving disquiet
Two raven hearts pecking at goodbye
Make a claw shape with two fingers and thumb
    with each hand beside your face
Tell-a-tale birds rage beak-necking
My chest rising and falling in hurried speech
I'm running out of breath   Say love   *make the sign*
Hello   can you hear me the way I can't hear you
The way I feel you inside me
    inside rooms filled with our belonging
Sign love   Three fingers waving like a banner
A branch holding up vestiges of *I'm here*
Lifelines hidden under two middle fingers
Palmistry laying claim   *This is me*   Is there a line
leading back to you   *Hold that branch aloft*
Middle and ring fingers arrowed down   rocking
    horns with the thumb sticking out   *sign love*
We're emotional caricatures
Which of us became the storm our wings soared
    raining an exposé of tears past
I can't hear the words tumbling from your mouth
Nothing lasts   Everything gets windswept away
I'm not the branch bending with the wind
My arm's heavy   Can I put it down

That symbol of surrender
  vomiting up a still beating muscle
When I refuse to even sign love anymore
Take your palm and lay it on my chest
You were there for every heartbeat

WEIGH DOWN

Everything leads back to this moment.
How a flea infested kitten's fur with

specks of dark feces, feels like a lupine
when it's penned inside an overcrowded

rabbit hutch. Thanks to Mama's unruly
fascination with breeding. Sand chigoes

flourishing beneath wired cages, blood
thirst biting my legs and arms while

I'm standing beside an outdoor washing
machine, pallet hoisted, spin banging

cowshit clothes. I feel scurrying jumpers
on my skin hanging wet laundry. I'm

begging for rain to drown the parasites.
Sleeping between infested sheets;

scratched raw, eyes shut tight when
a man strips my body bare. Rubbing

alcohol to soothe prickled skin. I share
the rabbit's misery, we can't escape.

Weigh down the darkness you keep.
And I'm kitchen stepstool squatting,

a few drops of Dawn dish soap in a bowl
of water; Flea combing Maine Coon hair,

wishing for Winter's cold reprieve. Nearby
a bucket to drown infested memory banks.

ANIMALISTIC

You only have to let the soft animal of your body
love what it loves. —Mary Oliver

There is nothing soft about me Mary
I'm all taut muscles   a counter force to effete
      Ice and glass are shattered by cold   Am I
Hide cured and stretched thin   pounded
The push back after the shove
Shadowboxing hope into malleable surrender
      eating crow   the dissenting saboteur
I'm the sentient punching bag   that feels too much
not enough   *Yet will split under the duress of trauma*
Tender as in yielding   as in lost resolve
Cut and dried like lamb's wool
      Which of us needed it more
A wilding removed from her wilderness
      while suburban sprawl devastates everything
Societies' forgotten Indigenous left on the roadside
The newest missing broadside stapled to a pole
Sharped edged as silica glass lightning fused
My jagged end's life blading forbearance
      There is no belonging in this familia of yours
Despair has nicked my bones brittle long before age
Even innocence abandons a child eventually
      This child to that man's stamina
Where is the soft in dying things Mary
What forge made you gentle enough to become
      succulent wisdom to be partaken   communion
I will give your innocence claws
I've seen morning dew glisten under first light
      while watching the shadows gather their haints
Words spoken from silent lips with tell-tale eyes

I fear the softness you speak of
        muffling what I've come to know
Some animals are all teeth and talons   meat-eaters
Some are prey   the soft animal
        my body has already been devoured
        by your familial things

II: Familial Treatise

NATIVE LAND

There was the flyswatter squashed
    to window wasp this morning.
Now I watch a different one hover page rasping
    close to my lap saddled book.
A floating storm with invisible wings.
Menacing giant ant body with a stinger,
    flying porch ceiling high between the panels.
    And disappearing from -
Eyes pleading for the company.
Sting me please. Leave grotesque bites.
I deserve more from this deadpan soul, not less.
Hollow the pain from spirit to skin.
Give my ugliness form, a reason to exist.
Remind me how I once wanted to carve
    my face with a paring knife.
Holy the unholy beauty vain men seek.
Come back, we're not finished.
My eyes bore a hole after the disappearing wasp.
Wait for the flying raptor parade;
I pretend to hear larvae crawling around a nest,
    skittering like rodents in the attic.
I want to get a ladder.
Glue my ear to where the wasp disappeared
    seeking the truth of a thing deaf ears can't hear.
Feel thin long legs drag my ear canal;
Pulp packing my eardrum.
Paper ash saliva honeycombed.
A mask built from bits of eyes, nose, and mouth,
    with high cheekbone ledges.
A gray paper-thin ghost of a head.
It's never quiet up in here now.
My tongue swollen silent.
No need for a body to lie still among dead flies.
In this belonging, I'm home.

YOU CAN'T HEAR THE LIZARDS CHEWING

We had moved to the land of baby dinosaurs.
Anole lizards and my brother's popping sunburnt
blisters, NY kids molting into FL
tatterdemalions regrowing our tails like gecko
Old neighborhoods and grandma's house
welcomed us back that summer to a world
full of lost and found friendships.
Familiar as the crotchet blanket covering me.
Donny and Marie Osmond singing *I'm a little bit*
country, I'm a little bit rock and roll, on TV.
As familiar as a kid's glee staying up late,
lights turned off watching a Halloween special,
fingers laced between granny squares pulled
up under their nose. The thrill of ducking under cover
with each throated scream screeching from 70's Zenith
speakers. Too scared to crawl out and turn the volume
down. Snuggled in, eyes squeezed so tight I'm seeing red
slushies from the 7-Eleven. Whispering, *Go to sleep*
stupid. Loud static burst shrieks crackling in the air.
Fireworks bloom in the dark behind my eyelids.
I'll get you my pretty! screamed the witch in my ear.
Breathing heavy with little kid determination,
I dared to peek from beneath the blanket. Garish red
shadows crawled across the living room windows
trying to get in. My scream is stuck in my throat.
I can't breathe. I run to grandpa's bed,
crawl under the covers shaking like a baby
woodchuck with a feral cat clawing at its behind.
I don't remember waking the next morning.
The fire had awoken everyone after feasting
on the front porch and it was entirely my fault.

It grew behind my eyelashes.
Never mind grandpa smoked like a chimney
or that grandma hated cigarette butts languishing
in ashtrays. I was the one who hid.
The ashtrays overflowed for days after
until my mother came for us.
Daddy stayed behind. You learn quickly
an adult's silence hurts; you learn
your fear has teeth and eats everything
around you. You stop being afraid because
the silence has bigger teeth. The only sound
you hear for the rest of your life is its chewing.

BLOOD BOILS A FAMILY WHOLE

We can't see the weight of festering want
Just out of reach   We taste
Darkness on lips tar sealed   honey stung
How do you hate/love
With a rope burned heart
Familial   brother/sisterhood   abandoned
        ethnicity scorched belonging
When a parent dies   Is it relief or grief
What remains   from distilled pain
Hallelujah   praise the distance between
        mothers and daughters who refuse
        to be saved in your God's name
Someday the call will come
Rib-caged shackled lungs screaming
Emancipation   tongues bit clean through
        sharpened on inescapable jagged truths
Can you see in your mind's eye
The cost to belong   Blood boils a family whole
Dodadagohvi—we will see each other again
Standing among hellfire's burnt religion
May your savior have mercy on your soul
Mine savors death with all my relations
Walking behind me   comfort me not

TRUCK STOP PREACHER

Hair teased and hairspray halo rolled into
a beehive with a thousand bobby pins.
Uniform starched and pressed,
hanging below the knee.
Slip resistance shoes, there's a lot
of truckers and souls to save tonight.
She's serving food with a side
of praise. Glory be his name.
"What ails you hon, I'll pray for you."
Don't matter if you believe, she's got
enough faith to heal your heartburn
and heartache. There's a pocket bible
in her apron with her order pad.
Leave a tip she'll throw in a prayer for free.
Who knew holy roller was a speed demon.
"Why yes, officer I did wait on you."
With a wink, he lets her slide.
Sins forgiven. God's got an eye on her.
Her uniform graces the floor by the door,
there's a dirty slip beneath.
Her children are wailing.
She's too tired to care, she broke her
smile on that last prayer.
She eats dinner without saying grace.
Her oldest is the fool for cooking.
Bible verse thumping headache.
Wake up kid, quiet your sister.
Truck stop preacher counts her tips;
There's a tithe to pay, pass the offering plate.
She's the donation queen.
Let God provide for her
children. She needs sleep
and the flock needs more sheep.

THE WEIGHT OF HAIR

Long down to my waist ending at the small of my back,
  Dark as a moonless night, moonlit blue.
I hated/loved those strands framing
    My jaw. Curtains shielding half my body.
A shawl draped over my shoulders
  Burying my face, hiding my pain,
    My too skinny waist and ribcage.
Hair doesn't weigh much at all.
I had so much of it,
  In my food, slammed in doors, ropes
    My little sisters twined their sticky fingers in,
      Pulling themselves upright.
My mother forbade me to cut it,
    Pentecostal or Indigenous reasoning?
    She blurred the lines so often.
When I would braid my hair,
    A chain traveled the length of
      My small body. Heat soaked, tying
    Me to a place and time I didn't belong.
My hair wore an ageist impression, native born/old religion.
  Samson to a mother who believed a woman's
    Strength was attracting god-fearing men.
Me and the weight of hair, her god cursed
    Me in so many ways, what more
      Could weigh my shoulders?
When saviors are scarce, a child will save itself.
Sixteen is a nexus between woman and child.
I part my hair in three sections
    Laced between finger's memorized dance.
      Right over middle, left over right,
    Middle over left, one link at a time until
      My braid/chain hangs tight
        Between my shoulder blades.
Tie it off so it doesn't unravel like a life.

Pick up the scissors.
At the base of my neck,
    I tuck my prison between the blades,
        Cut through until
    The weight of a mother's expectations
      Slithers to the floor.
I leave the braid for my mother
    Nailed to the wall
      And walk out the door.

MOVING FEAR OF STAYING

A child cries   *it's not fair*
        snot bubbling from her ruddy face
Friends are supposed to last forever
        don't listen to grown-ups
And home keeps moving
A girl becomes tree roots digging in
        searching for a safe place to hide
Where does a kid bury their heart
A room of her own   *wait*   she likes this place
Too late   here is where she shares a bed
Here it's cold and the oven door is always open
Here she can't breathe   *another school*
Bully the new kid   she's too quiet
        watch those fists
        she's made of spit and fire
Come sit with us   watch us eat
        her stomach growling *unfair*   *lucky you*
Girl unfriended   in a sea of ever-changing faces
All her addresses are one long never-ending street
        same state   different bed
        this one is blood stained
Which face did she put on for show   *good boy*
        this lie fits her tomboy figure
Forged in hate you and leave me alone
        She's forgotten every name he gave her
At home she's sister   daughter   temptress
Blame the child for what you don't have
        a home to call your own
        while his hands roam
The door is wide open letting in all the flies
        Truck packed with all her lives
They left their secrets buried beneath her bed

This is it   *Home*   They can stay awhile
A girl grown wild slips out the back door
        tears staining her face ruddy
Fear is staying in one place
Roots curled in on themselves   shying away
        when the door creaks open at night

LESS GODLIKE

I'm trying to be less
sharp bones and ache.
To forgive the girl on her scraped knees;
for believing every broken has a church,
while praying for a *do-it-herself* fix.
        Believing we're all,
Messiah,
        Yahweh,
                Jehovah,
wielding Thor's hammer,
striking down
        his creation/s.
        His children continuing in his *absence.*
(divorce dads at least pretend to
        make an appearance).
Our father who art?
So many names for one god, old gods, us.
What if I don't choose any?
A church of one with locked doors.
For god so loved the world,
I wasn't created in his image.
I was the cracked rib torn out of
        a monkey, dripping bone marrow.
        An imperfect specimen.
He made me a *NOT* you for a reason.
Pray for my salvation, please tell him despite
being omnipresent, he made mistakes.
Pick up his hammer, smite me in his name,
        or ghost a gun, make a bomb,
        pretend to be a Karen;
Use all your modern-day swords.
It's in your nature to wage war. Did you know,
Anger has a brother named Fear.
Blow after blow, strike that anvil,

        flames spitting, hissing,
        among my remains.
Cover your eyes, his glory blinds.
I should have warned you,
Cain had my eminence too.
Adam's bloody hands
        held the mallet.
I'm trying to be less like you
and your religion Abraham.

CONVERSATIONS WITH MY MOTHER

We have the same exact smile.
Except, my upper lip has a slight curl.
My *come at me* scowl.
Fist earned from speaking out of turn
Hers rips fake sincerity.
    Limpid disappointment in her eyes.
I don't think she knows how to speak;
Without an influx of *god* backing every word,
    Bless the child mom, dip your prayers in
    holy water for the accursed.
I used to think her beautiful.
We can't even look at each other.
A love like ours smells like betrayal.
Honeysuckle drowning in heavy musk.
My addiction drip line with no rehab.
I couldn't get enough of her fix.
    'I'll get it right this time' life dosage.
Take one bottle down, pass it around,
    there's a kid out here who wants your love;
    she's an offshoot of every mistake.
My redemption. Her savior complex.
The yearly birthday call,
    Are we saved yet?
My doppelgänger choosing her daughter's fate,
    lining up the stakes.
There's so much I want to tell you.
I believed varicose veins were lightning;
Thunder scars etched like tattoos on your legs.
I'm sorry, isn't an apology.
    My life wasn't yours to bargain.

Sacrilege is born in a mother's image.
I want to miss you.
We talk all the time in the mirror.
It's etched with a lifetime
        of conversations we'll never have.
I don't love you the way you love me.

III: Twilight's Lonely Cleave

NIGHT SPEAK

When you heard the rain tapping gently
        outside your window pebble tinged
A lover's insistent plea to be let in
Sweat draped in cotton sheets
        screen shifted breeze floating bare skin
Before your nail torn larynx's scream asphyxiated
Hatched spiderlings pouring from every orifice
Wool choked whispers misnomered sheep knowing
        want and desire are different beast
Squandering retaliation on forgivable regret
Who pays the piper to chase uncounted sheep
Delinquent soothsayer's childlike prayers
When you can't forget whose voice
        never shuts up
        in your head a familiar stranger
Memories sewn into a taunt fitted skin suit
        bloodied by touch   wail slapped birthing
And you want to pierce the heart of every white knight
        who failed to save the possessed maiden
Virginity's broken vessel has a female body
It's dark in the dark beneath ghost lids
The night spits up chewed morsels of cognition
Endless rooms in a house of woke with no escape
        every ex-lover is holding a hatchet of mistake
Our dank sub-duality drum grown quiet
Curtains tangled into knotted links of noose
Stygian slumber's bloated corpse awakening
        to sunrise's persuasive red-tinged cleaving
Dawn filters through eyelash ensnared brain fog
Do you remember a kindness of sleep

ATSISONVNV

All the ways we hurt
The 1AM me wandered
In the bone deep cold
Feeling the weight of added scars
I tell myself it's life
Emotional payment for living
Unliquidated IOUs for surviving
Asgina demands it's due
Rendered in pieces of mind
I stood among saplings stark
Against an indigo sky
Falling to my knees
Hands snow coffined   Seeking
Buried spirits comfort   crow or raven
Fallen from the sky in this crevice
Let nature take this burden
Feel the earth groaning   roots unfurling
It's a settled place
We are not meant to be bowed
Our hearts rib caged animals
How frail humanity
Without her woods
Close the doors
Keep the wild   from harm

WOLF IN MY BED

They say you bore three sons
  Hate Treachery Sorrow
    Hati Skoll Bjorn Black
As if you fathered human deceit
We place blame our fallacy on beast
You giant wolf tethered gagged by sword
An oversized pup by all accounts
  Destined to devour worlds
I'm your godless daughter
  living in the bowels of sons unmade
You bringer of darkness laying in my bed
Mangy warmth smelling of dank earth burial
Tuck me inside your sternum
  Hand thrust between ribs to touch lungs
    inhale exhale torment
I'll dance a gig on your tongue nick a vein
Bite down Fenrir Does revenge taste so sweet
  we would live out of spite
I am your mad dog silken ribbon deceived
Entangle me in the sound of a cat's step
 Woman's beard
  Roots of a mountain
   Bear's sinew
Fish breath and bird spittle
They magicked the earth to lay claim
I too wish for darkness
Lay your paw upon my brow
  Claws trailing down jugular piercing
Five delicate fingers stretching up
  to touch the blind nails of safe
Sing a guttural lullaby child abandoned
Breath deep dark of sleep wolf in my head
Our sorrows float rivers through men

THE CREEPING THIEF

Deathly quiet is spelled with
Four letters   D E A F
The creeping thief stole
My noise   snuck inside nightly
Covering my ears as if
I were a child who didn't need
To hear   descending quieten
Listen how closely
Deaf and Death rhyme
Speak the same language
A never-ending river flowing
Beneath a soul rendering
Quiescence   I'm not a meme
Deaf or blind   as if there's a choice
A suicidal pact with oneself
Locked inside a hollow skin suit   with a
Beating heart to hear   rib caged lungs
The sound silence makes
When nighttime—the La petite mort
Hollows out sleep's shallow breathing
Mining little death's conscious
On your deathbed what quietus
Will you find buried heart deep
I believe   the dead hear
More than the living
Silence is a wordless obituary
Deaf rhymes with Death
Does that mean I hear more

WOLF IN CAMOUFLAGE

I need to tell you something
That night was a hissy fit restless dark
My bed a drag sail   blanket whale
        spewing my body from its confines
Bare feet padding down the hall
I needed assurance the rest of the neighborhood
        slept a somber streetlight quiet
Tell me I should have known better
Do we ever listen to the waves breaking inside
My hand lifts a wood slat in the blinds to peer through
    a hallway window overlooking the pine fence
        into the neighbors *(the ones I don't like)* yard
        and their asphalt driveway   there   a dark shadow
A behemothic head arcs from the penumbra in my direction
        as if I too cast a silhouette that doesn't belong
It's as real as the cold wood floor beneath my feet
Quietly   not to alarm the skittish beast   I pull
        the blinds fully open keeping eye contact
      even as wood slats roll past my view
The deer and I stare at one another for the longest time
A raw ache for a wild kingdom lost   empty of forest
This magnificent beast out of place and time
He stomped his hoof once against the hard surface
        as if to break suburbia of its human slumber
Disoriented   I watch helpless as he swerves
Galloping momentarily out of view
        in front of the house below   careening
    up the road toward my house   nostrils flaring
Skidding to a stop   snorting   looking over his shoulder
I swear he looked up at me one last time
My heartbeat a windstorm of crows in a forest
I saw the wolf dressed as a man in camouflage turn the corner
Tethered to a Rottweiler pulling hard against his leash
Barreling down the road into the lot

above the creek where the deer disappeared
His flashlight beam strobing yards and underbrush
probing the underbelly of the night
In that moment I hated this man
Prowling the dark   a hunter without a rifle
Catching the scent of a wild thing   devouring serenity
A predator bird-dogging suburbia streets
After that night   I can't stop
looking over my shoulder either

PLAYING GOD WITHOUT A FLASHLIGHT

Fear and loathing eat days
Mares of night wearing faces of memory
  racing blind and trampling throated screams
Couch sitting on my hands wood paneled
Walls covered in *The Wizard of Oz* memorabilia
I'm Dorothy talking to an inferno head Pretending
  to be a wizened little man behind the curtain
Words flick against enamel escaping between my lips
All the house of me doors are unlocked
I've set a place at the table for you
Introducing each trauma sitting with us by name
I played the role of cowardly lion
  Empty as a tin man with no heart
A scarecrow psychologist panning my brain
Each response institutionalized textbook ready
You believed this yellow brick road
  led to all my selves
For years pulling up a chair to examine
  Each nag pulled from the race of my headspace
Time was a useful tool for thieving senses
Never staying longer than an hour
Refusing to turn on the stair lights to the
  basement's sublevel of emotional fortitude
Every other room mined of intellectual capacity
I never locked my doors you were free to leave
Your pissed stained road spiraled out of control
Munchkins couldn't brick enough winding yellow
Holding a motor purring kitten not Toto
I'm watching the ball you dropped roll away
There was never enough magical realism to forge
  the wilderness of me No matter how many times
  you stopped to skip stones across my creek
I own this darkness
The batteries in your flashlight are dead

SCRAPED FROM A BONING KNIFE

We're multi. Sum parts of homo sapient.
Seven layered skin suits, the topmost layer
Stratum corneum composed of *dead* cells,
Shedding barriers of pretend reinforcement.
Fillet knife the first three epidermis layers,
Pause the blade when you accidentally nick
Dermis the middling layer, *feel*;
Where nerve endings are housed.
Sense pain. Mounting pressure Anger
You will require a boning knife here in cutting deeper.
Stratum layered down to *bone,* scraped raw;
One on top of the other sandwiching Rage.
Fury. Wrath. Madness. Call it what you will;
I have suckled blood vessels and sweat glands,
Worried hair follicles thin but fed well.
Inside what Germans call my *haut, my skinned hide,*
Will and Hope bloodletting as if they were
Wrist sliced vertical in suicidal bludgeon.
My abuser, you with the five fingered
Closed fist of house broken *Love.*
Feeding child me, woman me too many doses of pain.
Did you know if you swallow enough it burns,
Boiled down to a feverish pitch.
If you siphon hatred through skin and bones
Long enough, if you gut punch your heart
Hard enough, in between all the layers of
Who you are you find
The will to live.

PULP

A single branch snakes finger spread
  from a heart in the shape of an oak door
Sprawled arm's length Twigs split a lone limb
A force bellows Storm shoved
  against the threshold
Appurtenant branches lightning splinter
  in answer boughs spreading wider
Cracks forming a winter Maple silhouette
Wood remembers how to bend wind coaxed
Bramble spire leavings litter the floor
Three fingered breaking at the stump
Thicket lathes bursting through pulp
Forest forked networks laced entrance
No wolf howl threads the night
  curdled tormented barks and growls
Rouged dark hair stake clothed in skin
  cracks the door's tree honed copse
A woman whispers greenwood won't burn
As a man stomps through
  her last chaparral of safe undergrowth
Staring out the window to the grove beyond
Wish to be timber tree trunk solid
  before chainsaw when we were
  sun warmed outstretched limbs
Before the door before man
Anger grew a tree

IV: Soft Animal

THEY WILL COME FOR YOU

Pick up a rock to skip;
Palm sized, mostly flat, wedged-shaped.
Not circular, more jagged.
This one needs to be heavier than normal.
Breathe deep the night air.
Swallow each inhale as if liquid courage.
Make sure you choose a dark night;
A new moon phase is best of all.
Strength is held between thumb and middle finger,
index finger straddling the edge.
Thumb on top as if you're trying to win
a thumb wrestling championship.
Pretend the rock is a baseball;
play catch, toss it up in the air
and catch it when it comes back down.
Play toss for a while.
You can see fine, the neighbor's floodlights
keep the dark at bay bright as any sunset.
How's your arm, limber, warmed up?
Plant your left foot. Line your shoulders up,
Eye your target. Aim. Put your body into the throw;
Smile. You're not skipping
stones across the sky tonight.
Pop. The lightbulb shatters. Glass raining every which way.
That adrenaline pumping through your heart?
Don't worry. Pick up another rock. Listen
to the night come alive as one by one
houses go dark and neighbors pour from their homes;
Ants scurrying to see who disturbed their hive.
You have a bag full of skipping stones.
Throw another and another, aim true.
When it's all over stare up at the sky.
Do they see this gift you've given them?
Do they understand now?

In all of heaven there is nothing to compare,
seeing the stars light up the sky, a universe waiting.
No longer blinded by porch lights, streetlights.
Yes, they will come for you. Remember this moment when
you decided to peel back suburbia's curtain
and freed the night-sky;
A gift once given can't be taken back.
Van Gogh, I finally see your stars.

CALF BAWLING MIGHTILY

I was always surprised they weren't all
        hides of broken bones
Tied up in the back of a truck cab
Jostled like sacks of potatoes driven
Across half a dozen fields before arriving

Each one bleating and bawling for mama
Mama roaring and running along the fence line
While adults whispered lies in my ears
We're saving them from the herd
Stronger   Better this way

My ten-year-old heart beats wildly
Along with the wobbly calf I'm trying to soothe
Both our hearts blended in a cacophony of fear
There isn't enough time to nurture either of us
Or the roles we played in this sundering

I wasn't supposed to care   There was this runt
Mahogany fur body with a muddy tear-stained white face
        a chestnut forelock between his eyes
Eyes pleading for mama in between bleats

My middle finger pacifier took a bruising
        calf suckled hard   And I silently
Name him   Curse him   Ember
For the flame on his forehead
Stepdad said he wouldn't survive the night

So many nights spent stumbling downstairs
Half asleep   Ember bawling mightily
Not hungry   Braying his loneliness to the night

Mornings after hay stuck in my hair   The little heifer
Fascinated by breathing   airborne condensation
Between us the chilly air

He grew strong enough to douse us both
        in fake milk froth   Blowing bubbles
Head butting the bucket and me
Both of us calves   Bucking the days

When the rain came   He stood at the fence
        staring at me   Fur soaking wet
In the doorway I struggled
        with waders   Lightning flashed
Ember's head twisted sideways
A burnt husk hanging from his splayed body
It's better this way I thought

The shovel head dragged behind me in the mud
Water dripping down my face
I buried the dead calf in a shallow grave
He wasn't going to be thrown in
        the back of a truck cab
The same way he arrived

I never named another one
And there were so many   so many
Bawling for their mamas

REWIND GO BACK

Mud and shit ooze down over
My forehead and eyes   Wild boar sow
Ramming the welded fence with her tusk
In my grip hanging upside down
The last of her squealing brood   Rewind go
Back to eleven-year-old me climbing
Steel squares one foot after the other
In way-too-big rubber boots   Pausing
Pull a boot toe loose from the fence
Leg over top rungs   Jump in the pen
Mama sow's wary eyes follow
I can't move   I'm mud sucked stuck
Nursing mama settles   Old man hisses
Hurry up before she finds her feet
My bare feet slip out from muck slick boots
I'm the fastest girl I know racing the wind
Shove a piglet down a shirt   Grab another two
One in each hand   Go little girl go
Mama sow flashes teeth   Leap   Fly upward
Toss the piglets over the fence
Hold tight one rung after another
Air hisses as a mouth clamps hard
Below my foot   I almost lose my grip
The fence leans precariously   tilts outward
A hand wads my shirt and hauls hard
The brittle grass   Sand on my backside
Smells like the sun   Warm pricked
I can taste salt   Sweat dripped in my mouth
My little brother running out of breath   Chasing
Frightened piglets dodging all over the place
The one inside my shirt shivers and whines
I hold it closer beneath my soiled t-shirt
Until I'm yanked to my feet
A rough callused hand reaches down

Grabs the piglet and shoves me away
Rewind go back to   I'm woken rudely
Before the sun   Scolded and shamed
Wasting time   Wild boars are feral
She'd just as soon chew your fingers off
I'll learn my lesson between pet and food
Let's see how she likes you after we
Take her brood   *Babies* I whisper
Rewind go back   to when you were free

BILLY GOAT AND THE TWO WOLVES

Televangelist Billy goat wanted to share
his Savior's amazing grace with *Natives.*
The sleeping giants were finally awakening.
Strutting like a turkey with an ace hidden in his tail feathers,
This shepherd was going to round up these lost sheep
using animal hocus pocus his friend shared.
He's a lion pacing the length of his den
'almighty' ready to smite the scoffers.
Wildly gesticulating he makes the peace sign.
All the oral history keepers in the audience lean in closer,
the reservation dead jostling behind
pressing against their backs eavesdropping.
There are TWO *wolves living inside of us,* he bows his head
hand over his heart, *The white one is good and pure*
The black one is EVIL! Which one are YOU feeding?
These wolves are at war with each other, thundered Billy,
face beet red, sweat dripping along his buttoned-up collar.
In the audience anger simmers into a collective gasp.
Someone shouts, *the wolves live in harmony*
another added, *they bring food back for the old and weak.*
To believe Billy, every 'thou shalt not' was a black wolf
And Christ the redeemer was dressed in a white hide.
Everyone knows wolves prey on goats. He was a crusader
for souls with a revelation of prophetic proportions.
His giver of tales friend was Inuit after all,
hold your horses, he's Cherokee. Same thing.
Behold the *1970's* televangelist admitting to folks glued to their TV's
it was a mere invention, a teachable moment. No harm.
A lie to all my relations standing behind me and lies accrue;
With these men's words in our mouths knocking against teeth,
while our tongues grow mold and dirt plugs throats
inside unmarked graves too many bodies deep.

We were the buffalo skinned for pelts and left to rot.
The language they cut out of our hair.
Brown skin clothed to hide us from father sun.
Force fed an Abrahamic religion we became nothing
    more than a Sunday school lesson in betrayal.
Every word gospel to folks glued to their TV.
Stay-at-home mothers mesmerized in their living rooms,
listening to the man preach about everlasting glory.
He's got one of us wild *injuns* for a friend.
Isn't he something spending time with *those* natives?
God willing their souls will be knocking on heaven's pearly gates.
Every denomination scalping the Indian into their western culture

Bleeding harmony out of the land while our mother cries.
In *our* stories, the wolves need each other. We're primeval,
    beginning and ending in the dirt beneath our feet.
Billy goat's two wolves marched
    to the tune of Jim Jones' Kool-Aid parade.

WHEN HUNGER

Eats away at apathy
Fleshes out your skin suit
    Gurgling stomach melt   Feeding
        Lies to an empty belly with what's left
When the unholy trinity of a man who beds
    Your mother before sneaking in your room
        Offers slaughter as salvation
    Hunger shakes your limbs like
A visiting missionary speaking in tongues
You hold the rabbit you raised
    The one that never bit you even
        When pellets were scarce
    Your favorite lapin with a mix of sable and
        Red fur along her ears and underbelly
By its hind legs upside down
Don't flinch when the billy club
    Cracks across the back of her head
        Just behind the ears
Let hunger explain away the numb
Stare into the trees beyond
    Mute the sound of the blade ripping
        Copper Agouti fur from flesh
For a stunned moment wonder did she know
Move in a trance   Blood dripping down fingers
    As one by one
        The hutch empties into a carcass mound
    And you wish you had starved
        to save the many
Days later clutch the salt tanned hide
    To your face and soften it with tears
        Listening to a man gloat about how
    He popped your butcher cherry and
Realize we're all prey
Hunger eats us alive

GIRL BAIT

Florida's salt tang wind stings in December
Stiff fingers indelicately untangling knots
No moon No light to see by
Searching out torn holes by feel
This cast net was handmade
His constant bragging told her so
In between belched words slow and lazy
There isn't a fishing license for lechery
She pulls the net over herself up to her chin
Sinking down into myakka—fine gray sand
Clawing deeper like a burrowing mole crab
Why choose a girl and not her brother
She needs more sinkers to drown
Thick shadows hide inside small hours
An angry kick her net cloak yanked free
Shaking girl bait loose from its moorings
The rock face's jagged edge is heel slipping close
Below the water lapping spume
Her shoulders know a cast net's singing weight
Looped over his left arm Lead rope in right
Shoreline waltz froth spitting stone wet
Receding waves suckling boot waders
She hears the sinkers' click gathered throat
The net opens a jellyfish swallowing night
She can always tell by the splash
Like a child who can't swim slapping water
It's never a good throw
Listen to the wind bellowing
Uk'tena the antler serpent strokes his ego
Pretend dad douses a child's flame
Everything goes dark for a girl used as chum
Descale her with a blunt knife

Before filleting   Let lightning strike
Hard glass   She can't even shatter
An empty stomach needs food
His is full of her splinters

HOW TO OUTLIVE A RAPIST

His living haunted like the dead.
Even after his actual death.
The carefree girl I was,
the woman I become, side by side
staring down at his gravestone.
All three of us no longer
wearing the same face.
Death cheated. We can't
get his stain off our skin.
Every breath we take trembles,
leaves wind surfing an open grave.
We stopped screaming for daddy,
long after our throats gave out.
She stayed with him; I grew older.
Today, both of us are wearing
phantom black and blue
neckties in his dishonor.
The girl loosens her grip on me
and fades back in memory,
back to when she skipped along
railroad tracks, arms outstretched.
I miss her, that part of me
who never had a chance
to test her wings.
I want the pieces of her
buried with him,
to sing to him in his grave.
Everything that hurt us
becomes a ghost.

V: Season's Betrayal

I APOLOGIZED TO THE CUCUMBER VINE

Snaking further and further into grass,
unfurling limbs from a hosed down plot

of earth; unentangling itself from its dirt
mates, and stretching toward yards end.

Fleeing the gardener, me, as if I held the
pruning shears solely to hamper its

rebellious streak. Sorry, to the tendril
curling indelicate around my heel with its

tender shoots; for stepping on protruding
limbs crawling toward the wild beyond;

Inhale the cut grasses warning scent—
beware humans weeding radish friends,

yanking stems from their mooring by the
roots. Hide under a canopy of wide leaves.

Sprawl until creepers touch chicken wire.
Climb. Trail after sunlight glinting off

hexagonal links. Wave to the tomato plants
tied to pikes. They're going to turn red soon,

blushing angry at harvest time, plucked
one by one. Whichever is reddest first.

String beans hanging around until they
snap. Even the potato plants are starting to

lean heavy pregnant with bulging roots.
The squash—blooming yellow belly

cowards. *I'm sorry,* is a poor excuse to a
sheared cucumber, caught slipping under

bent chicken wire. Gently lay
the twiglet spread eagle in the grass,

a sprig wraps around my finger.
Forgive me.

AUTUMN'S BONES

Tumble wind green leaf dance   tiny shadows
crawling asphalt and worried faces
Echoes of too soon spiraling across
    a Walgreens parking lot   Too bright
    last of summer sun glinting off a line of windshields
Needle prick a bark less Armageddon
Tempest tapping on the windowpane
Come you Autumn   whistle through the tree bones
of limbs raked of umber foliage   in this season
of dead things falling   Rattle your oracle bones
shake those pieces of ox scapula and turtle plastron
    of our human affliction   Listen to the creak and sway
As a Zephyr blows through branches armature grasp
for dark skies graying hope   Down   down we go   Below
the antler rut deer markings   Our sunless flayed bark
    buried dirt deep beneath the wind's moan
    to roots tangled in skulls of afterthought
Whispers rattling terra firma's rib cage
knees thunder cracked   floor mopped tears
Our hand wringing finger splayed remorse
    skeletons bemoaning the wind's rancid truth
Lungs long bleached of breath singing
come brittle soothsayer   Listen closely
as the wind speaks and the land talks back

DEATH'S CALLING CARDS

Twilight's aerial dark
Gloaming black winged sea
Starlings, Grackles, Red winged blackbirds
Tumultuous waves sky rise, tree fall
Between gluttonous blackening seed hoarders
Crows and Ravens lording the perch
A hum, a muttering, a rushing
Murmuration crackling sky
Soft flutter shush, autumn nightfall
Captivated dogs low growl watch
Hush, hush, you black beak sea of noisy
Harbinger's warning
Hoard fat, fly heavy against the wind
Winter prowls around the bend
Stay close, protect the many
Tonight shots boom the roost
Door flung open, ice slipping
I found death's calling cards cold to the bone
A Raven laying prone in a driveway
A Crow middle of road
To my knees I fall in headlight's glare
My brethren's tear stained bodies
Wrapped with care, feathers smoothed
Claws curled as if still in flight
Sing their spirits on, plead for mine
Autumn has come again
Cumulus fading quietus
The black winged sea no longer
Comes ashore at forest door
Only murmur to be heard
Is what's left between heartbeats
In twilight's silent gloam

FAIR TRADE

Unetlanvhi sgwanehlanv sgidolige
    Great spirit you are my creator   forgive me
Omnipotence doesn't make you all-knowing
Why did you give humans engorged lives
Your favoritism tripping over Elohi's tree roots
    drowning our voices in a gurgling brook of forget
There is no peace or equilibrium
    For creatures   great or small
Are we not all your children
Did you seek counsel with Ani Tsutsa
Sit at one of the seven boys campfires in the midnight sky
Listen to them speak of missing mothers
    while you scatter lives to the four winds
Childlike confusion   my grief   my fear
    trapped in the missing of one small spirit
Unetlanvhi didanetliyvedi *What will you trade?*
Barter with me if you dare
I'm offering myself up   all 78 organs
    a body's worth   206 bones and 32 teeth
You gifted humans with an overlong life expectancy
Unappreciated years spawned in ignorance
Of us all   wildlife are the gentler species
    And we take their lives without forgiveness
We hollow out our mother   oil her rivers of tears
    Burn the forest of her hair down to scalp for parking lots
I still have 600 muscles and 10 toenails and fingernails
Trade one nail for a bear's claw or a finger for a paw
How many years will an organ get me for a raven
I'm begging you Unetlanvhi   please
This thing is a hard carrying
All I ask from you is to spare one animal

And I will tuck myself deep between Elohi's dirt mounds
Satisfied for the bargain struck   this one life
        made into worthy bits and pieces
Just give me my damn dog back

SEASONAL AFFLICTION

A 7ft Douglas Fir tree which isn't even real
There's a galaxy   An Octagram polygon star
Triplicate rounded with metal cutout stars
Candescent north star haloing a tree cone in white light
Ceiling a blackout window cracked
Lost shards letting the light in or escaping
down the wall in a meteor shower
A secular evergreen bough   Pagan before our time
Conifer branches snow dressed Milky Way
a cosmic spectrum with hues
from seasons before burnt autumn
There will be no winter squall scratching to be let in
Giving season's multicolored looped branches
kaleidoscopic as a country's DNA
Each bulb a gathering of tethered moments
When the Fir temple shakes a house in December wind
Step off the stepladder to evict
a cat silhouette covered in pine needles
Watch out for the kitten's claws
Or the dog trying to bring a fallen branch in the house
mimicking the human bringing outside inside
I'm as confused as the beast
not welcoming a babe in a manger
Hoping someone will read this out of season
It's ~~Christmas~~ in July
There's a forest glen somewhere where evergreens
stretch their boughs beyond blackout ceilings
I'm not there

BY BELONGING

She believed ghosts inhabited the making of things
Anything once owned or loved became haunted by belonging
Inanimate want sticking yet another pin in reality's voodoo doll
Take this tapestry   newly stitched   haunt free
A gift yet to play a part in someone's life
Blue Spruce aida cloth stretched tight as a drum
    Ebony hues taking the shape of a black bear log sitting
        shadowed by a Tlingit native bear
    Twin spirits growling with each needle jab
Her bloody pricked finger   thumb rubbed dry
    Diluted ruddy smears left beneath stitched fur
There's a long strand of hair caught in a few stitches
She absently pulls what's left hanging   hers or the dogs
No one would know it's there but her
    the stitcher witching herself into fabric
Would they catch her scent where skin touched fiber
Inhaling a heady fragrance of Clearwood
    with cardamom and burnt tobacco notes
    creating a smokey barroom bourbon spilled aroma
The waft of campfire oil burning
Everything lingering in a room soaking
    into material   time dispersed
Dust motes air gliding sunbeams   settling everywhere
She wets frayed ends of thread with pursed lips
Her spit having kissed each knotted strand pulled taut
Dead skin cells spun between needle and thread
Laughter rebounding off embroidery
  like voices drumming the walls in a house
Spidery hands dancing by rote on an indelicate tightrope
    right cross stitch over left cross to make an x
In the serenity of movement she half smiles
She's sewn in

GOLANV

Tell me Raven how does it feel
trickster who magicked himself a bird
Caught in a net of human guile
Cunning intellect betraying the fool within
What did stealing the light from old man sky give us
He boxed it away to keep the dark
Perhaps it was not his daughter's ugliness
he feared but this world's This cruelty shining
a beacon on everything that hurts What is
seen cannot be unseen In the dark I can shed
all my skin suits like a snake Little girl skin
who grew up too fast The torn and bloody suit
inherited from a beating Why must I wear this flesh
of silence Put out the light so my eyes don't betray me
And you what of you to say for yourself
White feathers blackened by smoke Ember burnt
singing voice a mere caw mimicking humans
Creator gave you a single flame to warm the earth
At what cost raven hearted fool Scorched forest
due to humanity's belligerence Golanv you were
a fine teacher in ignorance and fallacy Then again
shiny objects have always fascinated you
my dear trickster Play one last trick if you will
Never mind ash flyer I'll ask Svnoyi—night
for his quiet dark Some things should never
see the day This skin grows too tight

WHAT THE LAWNMOWER COUGHED UP

I can see my breath cigarette billowed
Slipping around in navy neoprene mud boots
        I'm the neighborhood compost comedian
Mowing wet grass into a snarling chokehold
Leveraging the sputtering machine on an incline
        chewing and spitting up wilding grassland
Slender blades of grass bent over in supplication
Suburban crop circles with sunken wheel grooves
Seriatim aching shoulders   blistered palms
A gas hog's due for choking blades with wet lashings
Cumulonimbus rainbows   butchered
        with a sunbeam's carving knife
Revenge rides a downpour   raining a parade
Breathe deep the chill air   Stupefied by neighbors
        delirious need to cut nature out of home
Spring mows swathes of hurt   NY hands over April
Right before May's arrival without flowers
Inside my home   layered fragrances   comfort smells
TokyoMilk's Bulletproof perfume   skipped a shower
        Clove cigarette lip balm wishing for a smoke
Cloistered scents of safe sending hope spiraling
Catkins float the air like dandelion wishes
        Ostara's shuck and jive lawn masquerade
Season's haunt inside out   before the turn
I wouldn't trade dog breath for summer's quaking aspen
        fat bottomed leaves clapping merriment
When the rain returns   choke the lawnmower
        with grass-stained prayers   no one is listening

BOOKENDS

Look at his hands.

The before he sat down at the dinner table hands
with dirt under his fingernails, crusting palm lines,
in between fingers, encasing thick scars,
knuckle caked, and hard worn.
Feel her hard calluses after
finger tripping a rhythm ballet for hours.
See those hands curled fist tight
against a chest for warmth,
cardboard sleeping, street grimed,
fingernails chewed to the quick with worry
begging you to see past the dirt, to see
the person above the wrist;
The trembling, shaking,
fighting for a way through,
last-ditch effort, help me hands;
Hands wiping away tears after
a toddler's scraped knees, raising a street-
wise teenager alone, tired/overwhelmed hands
that don't know how not to love;
Aging, arthritic bent knuckle hands
with wrinkles folding in on themselves, and
wonder if those fingers could speak
what storied lives,
hard lessons would they share?

Hands whispering tales of body woes,
survival bookends, antennas in constant motion
asking you to listen, asking for a hand.

VI: Leave the Braid
(Abnegations)

I LOST JANUARY

A walk-in freezer of days
Keeping the dead fresh until Spring
With the sun's first breath
The sky turns the color of milky flesh
And January will always keep my dad
On a slab somewhere
Waiting for the ground to thaw
The frozen soil doesn't want him either
Veins more alcohol than blood
A walking pickled skin suit
All sour breath and rotting teeth
His body dead long before
If you count the stench of unbathed days
This never-ending month
All the holiday glut left behind
Hoarfrost skittering across windows
In this bleak wintertide blitzkrieg
Plumes of condensation escape my lips
An essence of me escaping him
The neighbor's slip and slide ice dance
A sad reminder like all memories
We never danced together
And every time I walk out the door
Each footstep cracks beneath my weight
Like all bones and promises
Much like a heart without a father
You have to be there to save someone
And kids weren't supposed to raise parents
I don't know where they buried him
Every January I pull up a chair to the table
In this frigid expanse of a month
His corpse still frozen

For once he has to listen
In this hollow ache
I tell him everything
About a daughter who's relieved
This macabre show is over

PALM WHISPERS

Tawny winged fury bashing itself
against mirrored sunlight.
Panic whirling off the bijou songbird.
The warbling churrs flight-driven
anguish to break through
a window's fibbed freedom;
As wayward leaves beckon,
breathless calm, don't hesitate,
quietly try to cup a whirlwind.
Be still little one with the
hand clasped twice missed plumage.
Finger caged, thumb opening,
warm palms holding a heartbeat.
Toothpick leg perch, pin-prick claws;
Bird palmistry reading a wren's future.
Weightless thrumming, waiting for
a closed fist, knuckle grip bone crunch.
Hands cupped open in atonement.
Peace settles quiet, trusting.
This soul weighs less than
a half ounce, more than mine.
There's an open doorway.
Hold out your offering
as it flutters, lightly dancing on
palm lines. Whisper, *Fly true.*
Wait with bated breath,
as wonder sits with hesitation;
Before wings spread wide, fury entreats,
and the wind breathes deliverance
into pine bough salvation.

RED DRESSING

Weatherworn   dress shaped fabric
        wind whipped   floating the breeze
Echoes hung from tree limbs
Faded claret cotton   polyester   linen cardinals
        Wingless beside a highway
Vacant necklines with empty sleeves waving
        to passing cars with blank stares
Bosom hugged tight   Hip snug   Missing a body
An unkindness of ravens flying above
        or a murder of crows black specked diving
The warm breath of a woman fills a dress
        slipped over her head   braids falling free
Warmer than brown eyes staring back
Flyers nailed with a native likeness
        Asking   *Where are we*   Meme my wisdom
          Murder my flock but don't you dare see
The native cleaved from an Indigenous child
        thrown in a schoolyard grave too many bodies high
History shifting the dirt over red bodies
Once   we were a commercial crying
        over garbage thrown from cars at our feet
Listen   the missing and murdered still speak
Howling our truth from the torn
        Remnants of red dresses
When did I become a mile marker
        striding the highway across nations

BURY ME GUILTY

My trust is so fragile, delicate as
a baby bird falling from a nest with
featherless wings. An egg a cuckoo
reared back its head to foist
out of home to lay its own.
Frail as an eggshell pricked by a raven's
beak and yolk tipped down its gullet.
Love wasn't weathered sea glass in brine.
It was hard knuckles shattering teeth.
Kintsugi pottery with gold glaze dripping
down between cracks was loved far more.
I have sharp teeth in my broken places
biting the hand that fed me. Fat fingers busy
wringing my neck for make-believe sins.
A church of one in a crowd pushing past.
Forgive the fist clenched at my sides.
Wafer-thin emotions gagging
on forgiveness. Bless the violence
father who art no-where.
There are men who live in the after.
I'm still wearing them on my skin
like an empty stomach devouring
a hungry child. An animal caught in a trap
chewing parts of itself off for freedom.
My existence, an eye for an eye in a world
already blind. For brittle bones buried dreams.
Survivor's guilt living in a gilded cage.
What rots inside me is everything
you forgave yourself for.
Trust never had a conscious.
Eggs are such fragile, breakable things.

BURNED THEATRE OF A TWEAKERS DEN

That night the neighbors left lights on after the sun
went down as if darkness were a beast stalking our
fear. We held our *Not me, this isn't a bad place,*
decorum close to home; as if the black bones
glistening after a hard rain was a righteous purge.
A blackened dollhouse view of burnt remains,
with a sore throat view in the roof, a gaping
mouth of rotten teeth falling out into a kitchen
sink. Human dolls with bobbing flashlights
playing "find the copper" game.
Moon silhouettes scaling a ladder
of broken. Hands, soot crusted
in someone's coal belongings.
Ash Wednesday palm readings,
repenting for charred homes or livelihoods.
They ravage as if the fire still burns, before
the game changes to *Operation.* Tweezer hand-eye
coordination retrieving, the drugs, the gun, without
waking Cavity Sam. They trade a red bulb nose
for flashing sirens. The morning after,
the smokestack dwellers slink back through
wall-less doorframes covered in snow.
It's anyone's guess if Mother Nature was trying
to gentle the fire's jagged fangs, graying
a three-story maw of pain. There is no purity
in this white, merely a temporary salve
against human flaws. Last night, I turned
the porch light off. No one needed to shine
a light on what went wrong in this living we do.

WHAT ESCAPES A THROAT

Listen. Open your mouth and listen
        To the timbre of your voice.
Wield the love, the hate, the ache which escapes,
    Like a double-edged blade wounding language.
Listen, how the caged voice sings.
Are you speaking softly, honeyed,
        Or with a smoky sotto voce?
Can we ask a stranger, someone close to you,
What the prisoner escaping your mouth sounds like?
Will they *say*—strangled? Thick with emotion.
Ask if the ruckus sounds dead, flat, or gravelly hoarse
        Inside harsh vocal prisons lacking affection.
Too loud and you're wincing,
    Too low and you're leaning into the shank,
            Straining against the silent encore.
        I open my mouth waiting for the slightest
        Whisper of unhinged locks turning.
I'm wound tight expecting nails on a chalkboard.
Tap the microphone a couple more times.
Is this thing on? Too late, my voice escaped
        Over the fence of awareness.
I can't hear myself speak.
A thief stole my ears one night,
        Starving for a bit of husky undertones.

MIGHT WE BE MAGIC

No sleight of hand   Tricks up our sleeves
Luminescent stars glimpsed between tree boughs
Fog wafts pretending to be early morning dew
Gravel crunching under footsteps remembering home
Long evening walks   Sky on fire   Day's dying embers
Discovering lost letters tucked in books
        when an argument still simmers
When everything that can be said is in the eyes
A season of letting dead things go   Burnt leaves
        Colder days and shorter nights   hurried steps
                Warm fires   Dank rot
Never feeling more alive   hedonistic
The sun's blazing gallop across daybreak
        in hot pursuit of insomnia phantasms
Crabapple tree's windswept petals
        reminding us old man winter snores
Rain collecting all our tears   rippling into a river's exhale
A red-tail hawk's wings shadow playing with sunlight
Arms holding love close and tight in a hug
        even when they are empty
All the unspoken things held in a smile across a room
Sun-kissed daydreams behind orange eyelids
Storm chasing kids on bikes
        lightning in their veins   thunderstruck pedaling
Wizened toothless grins accompanying a playful wink
Street signs daring you to pick a never been road
The slow roll of a car driving by a deer
        captured in its gaze beside the highway
The women who run with beast
        The men who swim their depths
Forest creatures breathing life into dead trees
All the rogue Animalia of our awareness
        holding life captive   What magic is this

LOOSE THREADS

Nothing ends where there is an ending
Something begins hemming frayed remnants
Nostalgia embroidered skin deep
Remembrance threaded sewn into days
Dates on a calendar flipping tearing
against machinated workloads
Minutes woven hours Seconds
knitted loosely Spiderwebs sticky with secrets
Catching us off-guard tripping over truth
Bitten tongue's unspoken words
Remorse tangled in a monkey fist knot
Forget-me-not flowers is Ancient Greek for mouse ears
Hippocampus strings of useless knowledge
Deciphering Index cards catalogued encryption
Memories backstitched over intellect
Sick of the same Repeat Mistakes
Bones with added flesh moth-eaten skin suits
Today wasn't promised yours or mine
A stitch slips loose drops
Unraveling yesterday's drapes
Starts and stops of wonder exiled lovers
Lantern stitching tomorrow tighter
Thread the film in the projector needle
Slowly advance each frame Cut and restitch
Watch closely Awaken to sleep
Emerge to collapse Exit to enter
Another door Opens and closes
Pay attention to the mending
Rewind Begin again Again and again
Slack threads pulled taunt
Last still frame Frozen in time

ACKNOWLEDGMENTS

Thank you to the editors of the following journals in which the poems of this book first appeared.

"Among the Missing"—*Palooka Magazine*
"A Name Is a Haunting"—*The Normal School*
"Say Love"—*Palooka Magazine*
"Harbinger"—*Palooka Magazine*
"Wallpapered"—*Palooka Magazine*
"I'm Not the Branch"—*Santa Clara Review*
"Weigh Down"—*The Rumpus*
"Animalistic"—*UCity Review*
"Native Land"—*PØST La Revue/The Journal*
"You Can't Hear the Lizards Chewing"—*Janus Literary*
"Blood Boils a Family Whole"—*IceFloe Press*
"Truck Stop Preacher"—*Colorado Review*
"The Weight of Hair"—*Grain Magazine*
"Moving Fear of Staying"—*Janus Literary*
"Less Godlike"—*Shō Poetry Journal*
"Conversations with My Mother"—*Anti-Heroin Chic Magazine*
"Night Speak"—*128 Lit*
"Atsisonvnv"—*trampset*
"Wolf in My Bed"—*Savant-Garde*
"The Creeping Thief—*Contrary Magazine*
"Wolf in Camouflage"—*Native Skin Lit*
"Playing God Without a Flashlight"—*Native Skin Lit*
"Scraped from a Boning Knife"—*The Massachusetts Review*
"Pulp"—*Pinhole Poetry*
"They Will Come for You"—*UCity Review*

"Calf Bawling Mightily"—*Palooka Magazine*

"Rewind Go Back"—*Colorado Review*

"Billy Goat and the Two Wolves"—*Contemporary Verse 2*

"When Hunger"—*The Temz Review*

"Girl Bait"—*Jelly Bucket*

"How to Outlive a Rapist"—*Native Skin Lit*

"I Apologized to the Cucumber Vine"—*The Rumpus*

"Autumn's Bones"—*Pangyrus LitMag*

"Death's Calling Cards"—*Hobo Camp Review*

"Seasonal Affliction"—*Ponder Review*

"By Belonging"—*128 Lit Magazine*

"Golanv"—*Jelly Bucket*

"What the Lawnmower Coughed Up"—*UCity Review*

"Bookends"—*The Lit Quarterly*

"I Lost January"—*UCity Review*

"Red Dressing"—*ANMLY*

"Bury Me Guilty"—*Native Skin Lit*

"Burned Theatre of a Tweakers Den"—*Native Skin Lit*

"What Escapes a Throat"—*Pioneertown*

"Might We Be Magic"—*UCity Review*

In Indigenous cultures, the tribe/community is said to raise a child. The same can be said for this book, for without the support and understanding of my readers and all the various editors, literature journals, and magazines who chose to publish me, this book wouldn't have grown into her cover.

I want to thank Chris Campanioni for taking the time to offer advice and friendship in those early days of exploring poetry. Chris's patience with a relatively unknown writer sending poems and words unbidden knew no bounds; his encouragement to submit that first poem is where it all began. I'm forever indebted for his guidance.

In the summer of 2019, Daniel Lassall put out a call to join a small poetry group outside of academia. The idea was to draft a poem a week to keep each other accountable. At the time of the invite, I had nothing published. The encouragement I received from Daniel and the group overall instilled the confidence I needed to become the poet I am today. Thank you, Daniel!

Thank you to Katie Lee for inquiring about publishing this collection. The idea and creation of *Everything That Hurt Us Becomes a Ghost* became a reality because you saw something in my earlier writing. I can't thank you enough for your guidance through every step of the making of this book.

This book itself is the product of one man's tireless feedback on every single poem I've ever written. Paul Underwood must have the patience of a saint. He stood firm with my endless pushback and questions, reading each piece with a deep understanding of who I was and what I wanted to say. Thank you, Paul, for this and for everything that remains unsaid here. You're invaluable to me. I'm a better person because you grace my life.

In all honesty, there are far too many people to thank for *Everything That Hurt Us Becomes a Ghost*. To every single reader, friend, and acquaintance that took the time to read a single word of mine—Thank you! For every single person that said, "Me too," after reading a piece I wrote; for those that are still trying to escape abusive lives; for those that don't have the words to describe their pain, their joy, their loneliness; and for all of us waking up each day with the courage to take a single breath: Thank you for being part of my tribe.